OPPOSITES

LOS CONTRARIOS

WRITTEN BY KATHLEEN PETELINSEK AND E. RUSSELL PRIMM
ILLUSTRATED BY NICHOLE DAY DIGGINS

A SPECIAL THANKS TO OUR ADVISERS: JUNE PRUSAK IS A DEAF THERAPEUTIC RECREATOR WHO
BELIEVES IN THE MOTTO "LIFE IS GOOD," REGARDLESS OF YOUR ABILITY TO HEAR.

CARMINE L. VOZZOLO IS AN EDUCATOR OF CHILDREN WHO ARE DEAF
AND HARD OF HEARING, AS WELL AS THEIR FAMILIES.

Published in the United States of America by The Child's World®
PO Box 326, Chanhassen, MN 55317-0326
800-599-READ
www.childsworld.com

A special thanks to Megan Fichtner, who helped provide additional
signing instruction.

Cover/frontispiece: left—Photodisc/Getty Images, right—Thinkstock/
Punchstock.

Interior: 3—Creatas/Punchstock; 4—Corbis; 5, 6, 7, 8, 10, 12, 13, 14, 15,
17, 20, 21—Photodisc/Getty Images; 9—left, 9—right, 22—Brand X Pictures;
11—Thinkstock/Punchstock; 16—Stockdisc/Photodisc/Getty Images; 18, 19—
RubberBall Productions; 23—Stockdisc/Getty Images.

The Child's World®: Mary Berendes, Publishing Director

Editorial Directions, Inc.: E. Russell Primm, Editorial Director; Katie Marsico,
Managing Editor; Judith Shiffer, Associate Editor; Caroline Wood, Editorial
Assistant; Javier Millán, Proofreader; Cian Laughlin O'Day, Photo Researcher
and Selector

The Design Lab: Kathleen Petelinsek, Art Director; Julia Goozen, Art
Production

LIBRARY OF CONGRESS CATALOGING-IN-PUBLICATION DATA
Petelinsek, Kathleen.
  Opposites = Los contrarios / by Kathleen Petelinsek and E. Russell Primm.
    p. cm. — (Talking hands)
  In English and Spanish.
  ISBN 1-59296-454-0 (lib. bdg. : alk. paper)
1. American Sign Language—Juvenile literature. 2. Antonyms—Juvenile
literature. I. Title: Contrarios. II. Primm, E. Russell, 1958– III. Title.
  HV2476.P4766 2006
  419'.7—dc22   2005027108

NOTE TO PARENTS AND EDUCATORS:
The understanding of any language begins with the acquisition of vocabulary, whether the language is spoken or manual. The books in the Talking Hands series provide readers, both young and old, with a first introduction to basic American Sign Language signs. Combining close photo cues and simple, but detailed, line illustration, children and adults alike can begin the process of learning American Sign Language. In addition to the English word and sign for that word, we have included the Spanish word. The addition of the Spanish word is a wonderful way to allow children to see multiple ways (English, Spanish, signed) to say the same word. This is also beneficial for Spanish-speaking families to learn the sign even though they may not know the English word for that object.

Let these books be an introduction to the world of American Sign Language. Most languages have regional dialects and multiple ways of expressing the same thought. This is also true for sign language. We have attempted to use the most common version of the signs for the words in this series. As with any language, the best way to learn is to be taught in person by a frequent user. It is our hope that this series will pique your interest in sign language.

Tall
Alto

1.

Short
Corto

1.

3

Hot
Caliente

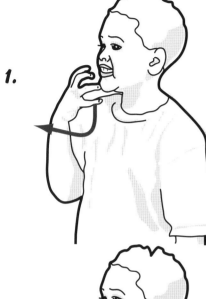

1.

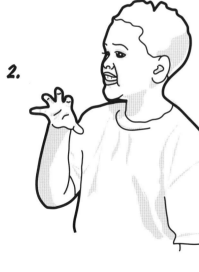

2.

Cold
Frío

1.

Pretend to shiver.
Finja temblar.

5

Fast
Rápido

1.

2.

Move arms right while hands close.

Mueva los brazos hacia la derecha
mientras que las manos se cierran.

Slow
Lento

1.

2.

Slowly move right hand up left arm.

Mueva lentamente la mano derecha
encima del brazo izquierdo.

Same
Iguales

1.

Different
Diferente

1.

2.

9

Big
Grande

1.

Small
Pequeño

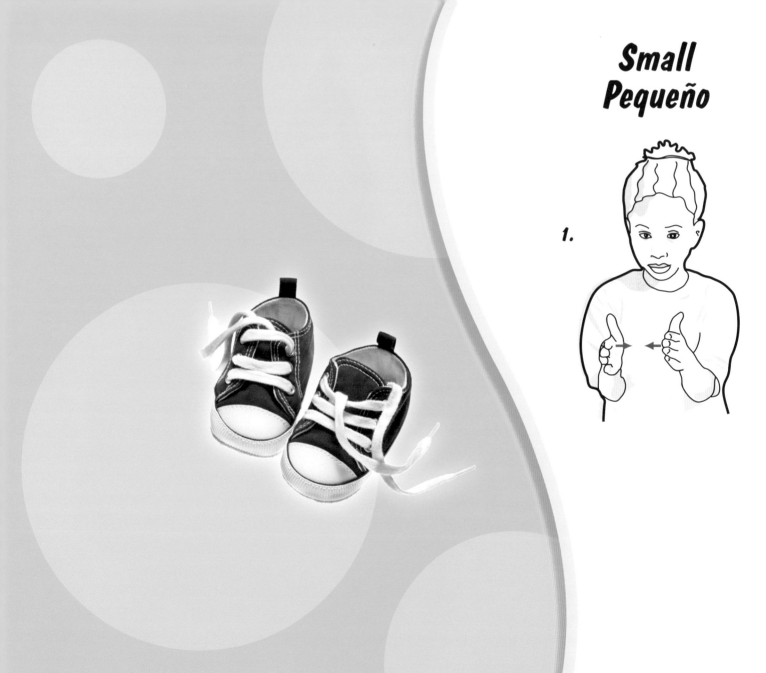

1.

Black
Negro

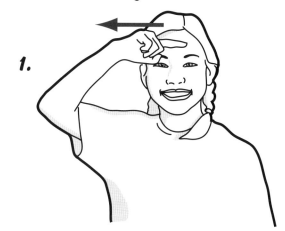

1.

2.

White
Blanco

1.

2.

Fingers on right hand close as
hand moves away from body.

Los dedos de la mano derecho se
cierran mientras que la mano se
mueve lejos desde cuerpo.

13

Left
Izquierdo

1.

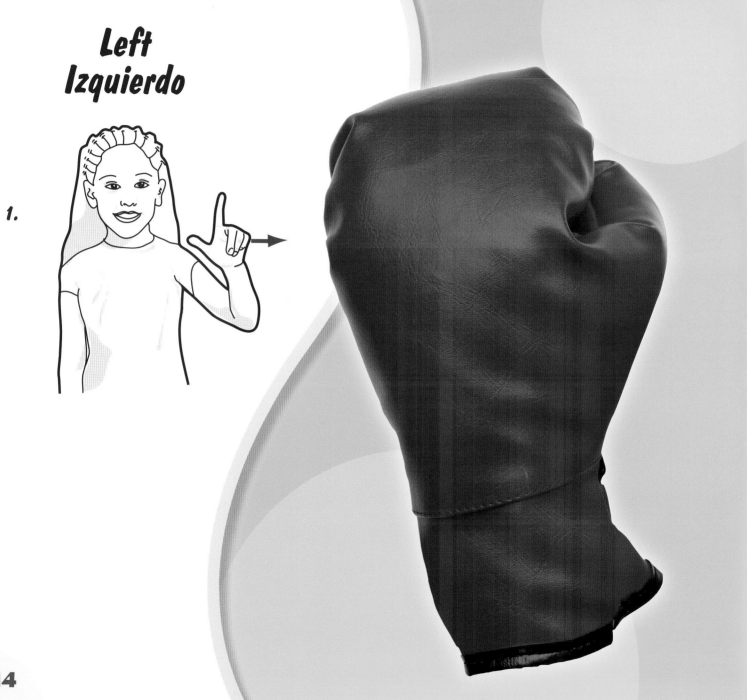

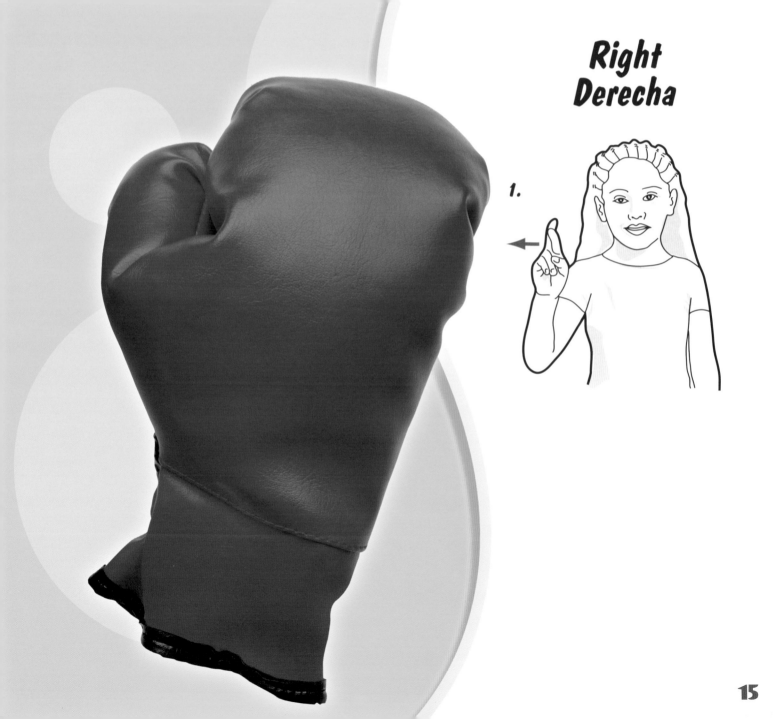

Right
Derecha

1.

Over
Encima

1.

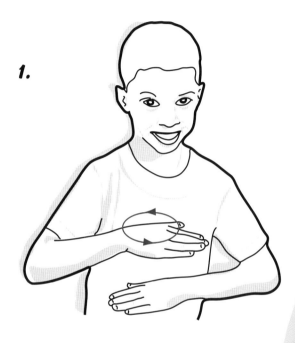

With palms facing down, right hand circles over left hand twice.

Con las palmas hacia abajo, la mano derecha circula alrededor de la mano izquierda dos veces.

Under
Debajo

1.

Up
Arriba

1.

Down
Abajo

1.

New
Nuevo

1.

Right hand moves over left hand and then moves up.

La mano derecha se mueve sobre la mano izquierda y después se levanta.

Old
Viejo

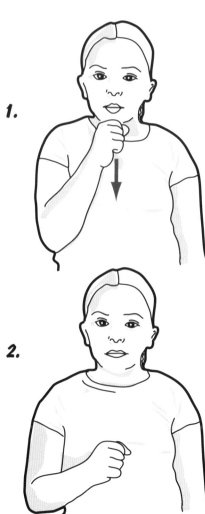

1.

2.

Right/Correct
Correcto

1.

2.

Index fingers on right and left hands point in the shape of the number one. Bottom of right hand taps top of left hand once while left hand remains still.

Los dedos índices de la mano derecha y la mano izquierda apuntan haciendo un numero uno. La palma de la mano derecha toca ligeramente una sola vez la parte superior de la mano izquierda mientras que la mano izquierda se mantiene estable.

1.

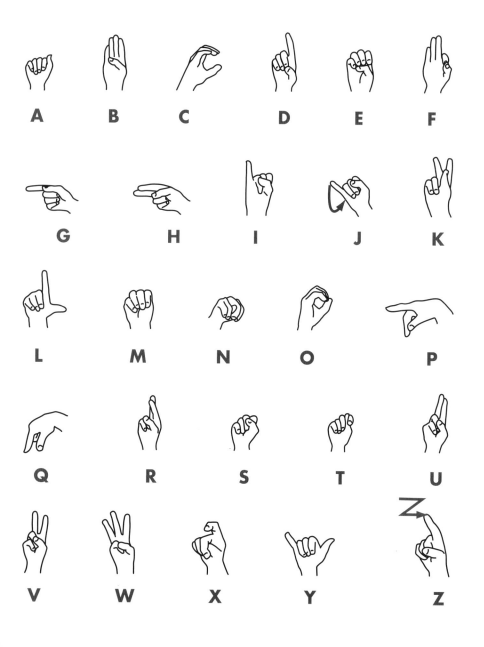

A B C D E F

G H I J K

L M N O P

Q R S T U

V W X Y Z

A SPECIAL THANK-YOU

to our models from the Alexander Graham Bell Elementary School in Chicago, Illinois:

Alina is seven years old and is i the second grade. Her favorite things to do are art, soccer, and swimming. DJ is her brother!

Dareous has seven brothers and sisters. He likes football. His favorite team is the Detroit Lions He also likes to play with his Gameboy and Playstation.

Darionna is seven and is in the second grade. She has two sisters. She likes the swings and merry-go-round on the play- ground. She also loves art.

DJ is eight years old and is in th third grade. He loves playing th harmonica and his Gameboy. Alina is his sister!

Jasmine is seven years old and is in the second grade. She likes writing and math in school. She also loves to swim.